The Fish that Ate Milwaukee

By Tracy Gustafson and Ted Datte

Illustrated by Sarah Brown

© 2023 Tracy Gustafson

Story by Tracy Gustafson and Ted Datte
Illustrations by Sarah Brown
Edited by Peter Gustafson
Schoolcraft, Michigan, USA

*This book is dedicated to my
father, Theodore Datte III.
He was filled with
imagination, laughter, and love.*

His fish tale inspired this book.

*With love,
T.M.G.*

"Tell me a story", begged the little red-haired girl.
"My favorite one about the fish!"

And so her Daddy began...

Once upon a time there was a boy named Walter who loved all sorts of curious things.

He had a whole closet full of treasures.
He had boxes of strings, jars of buttons,
and parts of his mother's old vacuum cleaner.

Although Walter liked playing with all of
these treasures, he was quite lonely.

There were no other children who lived near him, so Walter thought and thought about what he could do to get a friend. One day while he was swinging, a great idea came to him.

"A pet," thought Walter, "that's exactly what I need!"

A couple of days later, Walter's parents told him
he could get a pet, but that he must choose a fish.
Walter was very excited.

"Walter," said his mother,
"I want you to understand that
this fish is your responsibility.
That means you have to feed it
and clean it's bowl."

"No problem!" yelled Walter.

The next day, Walter's mother took him to get his fish. He decided to name the fish Piranha because he had read about them in school. He knew they had sharp teeth.

For the first few days, Walter carried Piranha everywhere he went. After a while, though, Walter grew bored and Piranha just swam around his bowl on the kitchen counter.

One day, Walter's mother called to him from the kitchen. "Walter, it's time to feed your fish!"

"I will do it later," he replied, "I'm making a spaceship." Walter did not remember to feed his fish, so his mother had to do it.

The next day, Walter was riding his bike when his mother called outside, "WALTER, its time to feed your fish!"

"I will do it in a minute!", he said.
But just like the day before, Walter forgot.

The very next day, Walter's mother grew impatient. "WALTER, if you don't come in here and take care of this fish, I'm going to flush it down the toilet!"

Walter did not pay attention because he was imagining that he was a pirate captain.

So Walter's mother flushed Piranha down the toilet.

No one could have guessed what was about to happen next.
Piranha swam through the sewers and into a stream.
As he swam, he ate tiny little fish and began to grow.
Pretty soon he was as big as a baseball bat.

The stream went twisty-turvy around the city and joined up with a river. Piranha needed to eat a lot more because he had grown so big. He was now as big as a bicycle.

At last the river opened wide into a lake. Piranha spent many hours there gobbling up all sorts of creatures until he had eaten every one of them. He had grown so much that he was bigger than a garbage truck. And he was still hungry...

On that very day, Walter was outside playing in his tree house. Suddenly there was a loud noise in the distance.

CHOMP! CHOMP! CHOMP!

Walter climbed down from the tree house and looked around. He didn't see anything but decided to stay on the ground (just in case).

When Walter finally found courage to turn around, he saw Piranha. He was bigger than the tallest building!

Then before he could run...

CHOMP!

CHOMP!

CHOMP!

CHOMP!
CHOMP!
CHOMP!

He was gobbled up by the fish.

And just as he told that part of the story, the Daddy swung the little girl into his arms and said "CHOMP! CHOMP! CHOMP!"

And he gave her a hug bigger than even Piranha could have given.

The end.

Made in the USA
Coppell, TX
13 December 2023